Culinary herbs

Cover: A collection of culinary herbs in pots.
Photograph by Michael Warren

Overleaf: A typical dry, sunny habitat of aromatic herbs in the Mediterranean region. Rosemary (*Rosmarinus angustifolius*) growing wild in Corsica.
Photograph by Martyn Rix

Culinary herbs

A Wisley handbook

Mary Page

William T. Stearn

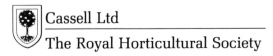

Cassell Ltd

The Royal Horticultural Society

Cassell Ltd.
1 Vincent Square
London, SW1P 2PN
for the Royal Horticultural Society

First published 1974
New edition, fully revised and reset 1985

British Library Cataloguing in Publication Data
Page, Mary
  Culinary herbs.
  1. Herbs
  I. Title   II. Stearn, William T.
  641.3'57   TX819.H4

ISBN 0–304–31080–8

Line drawings by Victoria Goaman
Photographs by Martyn Rix, William T. Stearn, Michael Warren
Design by Kwan Brenchley

Typeset by Georgia Origination Ltd., Formby
Printed and bound in Spain by Artes Graficás Grijelmo, Bilboa

Contents

Culinary Herbs

INTRODUCTION

From remote times onwards people have sought to vary and enliven the flavour of their monotonous staple foods or to disguise the unpleasant taste of food no longer fresh by adding pungent herbs and spices, these being not necessarily pleasing in themselves but imparting relish and diversity when used moderately. Such plants, with distinctive smells and flavours, mostly inhabit rather warm and seasonally dry regions; thus the maquis-covered hillsides of the Mediterranean region abound in aromatic shrubs and herbs; from here have come the bay laurel, coriander, rue, sage, savory and common thyme. Many such redolent Mediterreanean plants are quite unpalatable but presumably by trial and error the cooks of Ancient Greece and Rome discovered the gastronomic qualities of the select few, a knowledge which has passed down to us. There is manifestly a continuity between the kitchen and herb gardens of classical times, those of medieval Italy, the monastic gardens of northern and central Europe and our modern gardens. The names of many herbs still attest their southern and indeed their classical origin, taking their continuous cultivation back over two thousand years. Thus our English name for 'rue' is from the Latin *ruta*, 'sage' from *salvia*, 'parsley' from Greek and Latin *petroselinon*, 'fennel' from *foeniculum*, 'savory' from *satureia*. Mints (Latin *menta*, Greek *minthe*) grow wild over much of Europe, but seemingly their culinary value was first appreciated in Greece and Italy. Other lands have also contributed: garlic for example had its origin in central Asia, Chinese chives in China, tarragon in southern Russia, lemon verbena in South America.

Adapted mostly to a Mediterranean type of climate, these herbs thrive best and keep their flavour strongest as a rule when grown in well-drained soil in a sunny place.

The herb garden of former times, as Boulestin and Hill have said, was 'a well ordered collection of *materia medica*, which supplied the household not only with pot herbs, but with Cough Mixtures, Tonics, Sweet Waters, Love Potions, Insect Powders and Cosmetics', in fact with most of the preparations that we now obtain ready made from the chemist. It was strictly utilitarian and, though it is quite possible to reproduce it, we must not expect that an exact reproduction will add much beauty to the garden. But most people who make 'an old herb garden' are wisely content to create a graceful illusion of antiquity with a few typical and decorative plants, such as rue, rosemary, balm and marigold, which group well together and fit into their modern setting, like an old sampler, with the slightly decadent charm of 'a faded romanticism'. They derive an unobtrusive attractiveness from their contrasting leaf-shapes and their varied shades of green rather than from their flowers which are mostly small and pale.

The aim of the present concise handbook is, like the old herb garden, strictly utilitarian and practical. It omits most of the herbs of medicinal repute traditionally included in books on herbs and herb gardens (see p.63) and deals almost exclusively, though not exhaustively, with the herbs from the outdoor garden which can be used in the kitchen either for spicing foods or as additions to salads. These are variously known as culinary herbs, condiment herbs or pot herbs. The volatile oils of most of these plants are contained in minute glands on the leaves or stems or within

Lemon balm (*Melissa officinalis*), a herb from which a refreshing drink can be made (see p.29).

canals inside the leaves and fruits; the sulphur compounds giving onions, garlic, chives, horseradish etc. their pungent smells are formed after injury by cutting or bruising. Thus the purpose of chopping and pounding herbs in the kitchen is to liberate these aromatic substances from their containers in or on the plant.

Such herbs used carefully add flavour to processed and deep-frozen foods just as in former times they made more palatable the meat preserved for winter by salting. As most herbs have a strong flavour only small quantities should be added until the seasoning of a dish has been approved. Chervil, chives, mint and parsley should be used fresh. Others, such as bay laurel, lemon verbena, rosemary, sage and thyme, retain much of their distinctive flavour when dried and can be stored in glass jars for winter use. The quantity of pepper and spices can be reduced when basil, marjoram, summer savory and thyme are used. Lovage and the above herbs also make it possible to cut down the use of salt, which may be helpful to sufferers from heart or kidney trouble. Sweet cicely, lemon balm and angelica added to acid fruits such as gooseberries, red and black currants reduce the quantity of sugar needed and impart a new flavour. Lemon balm, peppermint and rosemary infused in boiling water make refreshing drinks either alone or added to China or Indian tea.

COOKING WITH HERBS

Most cookery experts agree that far too little use is made of herbs in English cooking, and where they are used the choice is often restricted to a very limited range; however, in recent years, cookery writers, such as Elizabeth David, have done much to encourage the more general use of herbs. The twenty or so herbs described in this booklet can easily be grown in most gardens and interest and variety added to many dishes by the discriminating use of them. There are many excellent cookery books giving a great variety of recipes using herbs; it is not the function of this booklet to include recipes in detail and only general guidance is given. There are no hard and fast rules; personal taste and experiment will determine the selection and amounts of each herb to be used.

Herbs can easily be introduced into simple everyday cooking and not only in the more elaborate dishes. All that is needed is the addition of sprigs or finely chopped young leaves, either singly or in a mixture; e.g. basil, fennel, mint, parsley, rosemary and tarragon are frequently used with other herbs as they have the property of bringing out their flavour. A regular supply of suitable young growth can be maintained throughout the growing season by continuous cutting out of the older shoots, and for winter use herbs may be harvested and dried or stored in the freezer; details are given in a later section. The quantity to use is often puzzling to a beginner and greatly depends on individual taste, but it must be stressed that over-use of herbs can dominate and spoil the basic flavour of food instead of enhancing it. For chopped fresh herbs one heaped tablespoon is generally recommended for a dish for four persons; dried herbs are so much more concentrated that only half or even a third of this amount should be sufficient. If they are to be removed before serving they can be tied up in a piece of muslin, or if sprigs are used they should be tied into a small bunch, leaving a long thread so that they can easily be pulled out. Some recipes call for a *bouquet garni*; this consists of two or three leaf-stems of parsley (which have the strongest flavour), a sprig of marjoram and thyme and a small bay leaf; various other such bouquets can be made to taste. Basil, with its rich spicy flavour will add a subtle new taste if chopped and sprinkled over chops or joints of chicken, lamb, pork or veal before roasting. Sprigs of rosemary can be laced into the skin of a joint of lamb, and tarragon is particularly delicious with chicken, a small bunch being placed in the cavity before cooking and finely chopped leaves added to the gravy. Bergamot leaves used whole on a roasting joint of pork make a pleasant change from the more commonly used sage. Mixed herbs can be added to give extra flavour to casseroles and stews as well as being used in sauces, soups and stuffings and for garnishing.

The use of herbs with vegetables need not be limited to the traditional mint, parsley and chives. Dill and fennel can be cooked with any of the brassicas to make them more digestible, and basil, mint or thyme will add interest to the somewhat insipid marrow. Chopped young leaves of angelica, basil, chervil, chives, lemon balm, parsley, salad burnet and sweet cicely add piquancy to green salads and the just emerging shoots of lovage make a good substitute for celery. Fennel and dill are also useful to counteract the richness of oily fish such as herrings or mackerel, and herbs can be used to flavour egg dishes and cream cheese. Herb bread and scones are becoming increasingly popular.

Herb jellies for serving with meat, such as sage jelly with pork and poultry, can be made from various herbs, e.g. mint, rosemary, sage and thyme, by first pouring boiling water over them to make an infusion, to which, a quarter of an hour later and after straining them through a cloth, lemon juice and honey are added. When this syrup has been brought to the boil, the addition of pectin will make it set as a jelly when poured into hot glass containers.

Some herbs, such as dried lemon verbena, mints and rosemary, can be used in potpourris.

Below: *Thymus vulgaris*, the common thyme, a useful constituent of a *bouquet garni*.

Far below: *Ruta graveolens* 'Jackman's blue', a herb grown mainly for its attractive appearance.

CULTIVATION

The cook's convenience is best served by growing herbs near the kitchen. Too often a gardener husband keeps herbs growing in a somewhat remote part of the garden which his busy wife ignores. Most of them should be grown in a sunny place in well-drained soil. This suits the hardy perennial shrubs or shrublets such as rosemary, rue, sage and thyme and the tender annuals such as basil and sweet marjoram. The young growth so necessary for the pot can be obtained by cutting back only part of a bush, thus not spoiling its decorative aspect.

Mints, which are aggressive spreaders, prefer moister positions. Horseradish likes a deep rich soil. Plants such as these endanger less vigorous herbs, such as chives and thyme, and should be given space in the kitchen garden or an odd corner where they can do no harm.

Those whose garden space is limited can grow a selection of herbs in tubs and large pots on a balcony or patio. Ideally such containers should be about 12 inches (30 cm) deep, although small herb plants can be grown in window boxes only 6 to 8 inches (15 to 20 cm) deep. The soil and the plants in the larger containers may need to be changed every 4 to 5 years and in the shallower window boxes renewal may be necessary every year, this work being carried out in spring. Drainage holes in the containers must be covered with metal gauze or broken pieces of clay flower pots placed concave side downwards and covered with a layer of fibrous material such as leaf mould or peat. The containers are then filled to within an inch (2–3 cm) of the rim with a good, well-drained compost. They need to be raised from a flat surface on tiles or small stones to facilitate drainage. Parsley pots form an elegant means of having parsley close at hand, and 'tower' pots are likewise convenient in providing opportunity for growing many herbs in a small space.

Rosemary, sage and sweet bay can be grown satisfactorily in the larger containers placed in a sunny position. Mint and tarragon could also be grown but need some shade and plenty of water in hot weather. Chervil, chives, parsley, savory and thyme are suitable for smaller containers and window boxes.

Growing herbs indoors will only be successful if they are given very good light and the plants and soil are renewed frequently. The selection will need to be limited to the smaller plants.

Methods of propagation depend on the nature of the plant. Annuals and biennials or plants treated as such, e.g. basil, borage, chervil, dill, fennel, sweet marjoram, parsley, summer savory, must be raised from seed, the time of sowing depending on the hardiness of the species as noted under each. Parsley germinates slowly and is sown from April onwards to August. Chervil can be sown any time, but preferably in late summer to give a crop of leaves in spring. Basil and sweet marjoram, being frost-sensitive, are best sown in May. In general April and May suit most herbs raised from seed.

Perennials with rhizomes or forming clumps, such as chives, horseradish, lovage, mints, sweet cicely, tarragon and thyme, are propagated by division in spring or autumn, although clumps of chives or Chinese chives can be lifted and broken into small tufts at any time from spring to autumn.

Shrubs or shrublets, such as bay laurel, rosemary, rue, sage and lemon verbena, are propagated by cuttings.

Many herbs are stocked and kept available to the general public only by a few specialist nurseries, and these should be supported by buying from them.

DRYING HERBS

Whenever possible, herbs should be used young and freshly gathered. Almost always their aroma is much stronger than that of the dried product, although freeze drying is proving as success-ful with herbs as with other garden produce. Home-dried herbs will be in a better condition than those purchased from a store, provided that a few but essential details receive attention. Herbs should be gathered early in the day as soon as the dew has dried and before the hot sun has dispersed any of the valuable volatile oil. The shoots will contain a maximum of oil immediately before they flower; the best material is gathered then. They should be cut with a sharp tool and put into a shallow basket; damage caused by using blunt knives or by bruising will result in loss of aromatic oils. If the herbs are dusty they should be dipped in cold water and carefully dried with a soft cloth. Drying must take place in the shortest time possible in moderate heat and with a free circulation of air; all sunlight must be excluded, otherwise the colour of the finished product will be spoilt. Small herbs, such as thyme and marjoram, are usually spread in a thin layer on a muslin-covered rack and large herbs, such as sage, are usually tied in small bunches and suspended from a beam so that air circulates freely around them; an electric fan will provide a current of air essential for rapid drying.

Small quantities of herbs can be dried on the rack which is so often fitted above a cooking stove, once cooking has finished and before the stove is cold. An airing cupboard with the door left open for ventilation or an attic with the roof window covered usually has convenient beams from which bunches of herbs can hang. The average temperature required varies from 80° to 100°F (26.5° to 38°C).

When the leaves are brittle and break easily the product is ready to store. The leaves should be stripped from thick, tough-stemmed herbs, but not from small ones such as thyme; then they are rubbed into small flakes (like tea), but not to a dust-like powder. Darkened screw-cap bottles are ideal for storage as the finished product must be kept completely dry and all light must be excluded; the filled bottles are then stored in a dry, dark cupboard. Dried herbs should never be stored in paper bags or in plastic containers; the former absorb the aromatic oils and the latter are not suitable as the contents tend to 'sweat'. Waxed cartons are suitable provided these can be properly sealed.

Below: Many herbs will grow happily in pots, especially the 'parsley pots' shown in this picture.
Opposite, above: Winter savory, *Satureja montana*, a woody perennial. The golden leaves are of variegated lemon balm.
Opposite, below: Two forms of Basil, *Ocimum basilicum*, a plant which is grown as an annual in Britain. Shown here are the purple-leaved and narrow-leaved forms.

Herbs can also be preserved for winter use by freezing. This method is quicker and the essential oil and natural green colour are better retained than by the drying process. It is not usual to blanch the herbs unless storage is to be prolonged. Various methods can be used. Small bunches of single herbs or *bouquets garnis* can be tied up and spaced out on a flat tray for freezing; once frozen they should be stored in rigid containers in the freezer as frozen herbs are extremely brittle. Another method is to add a bunch of herbs used with a particular vegetable (such as summer savory with beans or mint with green peas) to the vegetable before freezing it. Chopped herbs can be packeted in small envelopes of freezer foil, which are then sealed and frozen, or packed into the sections of ice cube trays and covered with water. When frozen these cubes can be removed to a larger container for storage.

As herbs have a strong odour even when frozen the containers in which they are stored must be airtight; otherwise other foods may pick up their aroma. Careful labelling is essential as herbs are difficult to identify after they have been frozen.

LIST OF PRINCIPAL CULINARY HERBS

Angelica
Angelica archangelica L   Umbelliferae (Apiaceae)
Angelica merits a place in the garden for its appearance as well as its uses, although it needs a lot of space. It is a robust, short-lived perennial with branching flower stems up to 8 feet (2.5 m) and large light green basal leaves which will easily occupy an area 5 feet (1.5 m) across. The leaves are divided into numerous sharply toothed segments, the terminal one being usually three-lobed: the small very numerous greenish or creamy white flowers are in rounded heads about 4 to 6 inches (10–15 cm) across. It is a native of central and northern Europe, even extending into the Arctic, and has become naturalised in Britain and elsewhere as a garden escape. When bruised it has a distinctive aromatic pleasant scent.

Candied angelica is prepared from young stems and fleshy leaf stalks. Candying can be done at home by the normal method but this is a very lengthy task. A quick method is as follows. Tender stalks or leaf stems only should be used; these will be available in early summer. Cut into 3 to 4 inch (8–10 cm) lengths, place in a pan with sufficient water to cover, bring to the boil, simmer until tender and bright green, and dry in a cloth. Then put into a pan with 1 lb. (45 g) sugar to each pound of stalks, cover and leave for two days, bring slowly to the boil and continue to boil gently until the angelica is transparent and green. Drain in a colander, toss in caster sugar and allow to dry off in a cool oven (250°F–120°C) before storing in a screw top jar. Young tips and leaf-stalks can be cooked with rhubarb and gooseberries to counteract their tartness; the usual recommendation is 1 oz of fresh angelica to each $\frac{1}{2}$ lb of fruit. The seeds provide an oil used in Benedictine liqueurs.

Angelica thrives best in a shady place on moist but well-drained soil. The plant may take up to four to five years to flower and ripen seed, and will then die leaving an unsightly gap in the border. To overcome this problem a younger plant should be grown nearby to take its place. The seed loses its vitality quickly and therefore should be sown as soon as ripe; once established, however, it may produce an excessive number of self sown seedlings. (see p. 35)

Basil
Ocimum basilicum L.   Labiatae (Lamiaceae)
Basil, probably a native of south-eastern Asia, has been cultivated in Europe for some two thousand years and esteemed as a medicinal and culinary herb on account of its spicily fragrant leaves which impart a distinctive flavour to soups, salads, stuffings, sausages, egg, fish and cheese dishes etc. and are now virtually essential in many Italian dishes. It is particularly valuable for use with any dish containing tomatoes, e.g. finely chopped and sprinkled over sliced tomatoes for a salad or in sandwiches, or used as a flavouring in tomato juice, puree or sauce. A popular variation of *O. basilicum*, sometimes known as 'Dark Opal' or 'Purpurascens', has purple stems, leaves and flowers, and is a decorative garden feature. There is also a variant with large crisped leaves, sometimes known as 'Lettuce Leaf', another with very compact growth and small leaves known as "bush basil" or 'minimum' and another with a lemon scent known as 'citriodorum'.

A perennial in warm countries, basil has to be treated as a tender annual in Britain and rarely attains here its possible height of 2 to 3 feet (60 to 90 cm). It makes a low much-branched bushy plant with glossy light green ovate leaves up to 2 inches (5 cm) or so long. The white or purple-tinged flowers are $\frac{1}{3}$ to $\frac{1}{2}$ inch (1 to 1.3 cm) long.

Basil is grown commercially on a large scale in many warm regions, notably California, the leaves being dried for culinary use or used fresh for extraction by steam distillation of the oil used in perfumery. In Britain it is best sown in a cool greenhouse or frame in April and planted out in a warm protected sunny position in well-drained soil. Root disturbance stunts growth; hence it is usual to sow a pinch of seed in a 3-inch pot, thinning to 2 or 3 plants, potting on if necessary until the outdoor garden is frost-free. To encourage a bushy habit the tips should be pinched back in the course of gathering. For pot cultivation, under glass, the less aromatic bush basil (*O. minimum L.*) about 6 to 12 inches (15 to 30 cm) high, with leaves to $\frac{3}{4}$ inch (2 cm) long, is preferable on account of its compact growth.

A winter supply of fresh basil can be maintained by lifting plants from the garden in early September with the minumum of root disturbance, potting them in a well drained fibrous compost and growing them on a window-sill in the house in a good light. Frequent cutting of the terminal shoots will be necessary to keep the plant compact and bushy.

Bay

Laurus nobilis L.   Lauraceae

Bay, also known as sweet bay or bay laurel, is the original laurel of the Greeks and Romans from which they made wreaths to crown distinguished men. It should not be confused with the poisonous cherry-laurel (*Prunus laurocerasus* L.). A leaf of cherry laurel is dark and opaque when held up to the light with only the main side-veins visible and has no marked smell when broken, whereas a bay leaf held against the light displays an intricate network of translucent veins and veinlets and has a pungent spicy aroma when broken. Bay leaves are elliptic, smooth, dark green above, light green below when fresh, wedge-shaped at the base, long-pointed at the tip, with short reddish stalks.

Although this evergreen tree is a native of the Mediterranean region, it is surprisingly hardy in southern England and, even when killed almost to ground level in an exceptionally severe winter, it will usually shoot again with vigour from the base. It makes a densely foliaged tree up to about 40 feet (12 m) high from which leaves can be picked whenever required. The creamy yellow flowers which appear in clusters in the leaf axils in early spring are conspicuous by their numerous stamens and are followed in hot summers by dull purple fruits.

Bay is frequently grown in tubs and is not damaged by clipping; during severe weather such a shrub can be brought indoors. It is propagated by cuttings using half-ripe shoots taken in July, August or September as they become firm. After the lower leaves have been removed dip the ends in a rooting compound and insert in a sandy soil in a cold frame. Rooting should have taken place by the following September.

Bay leaves should be dried slowly in shade and then stored in tightly sealed glass jars. As the essential oil is very strong bay leaves are never pulverized but merely cut or cracked before being added to food. They are commonly used with fish cooked in

Borage, *Borago officinalis*, a plant grown chiefly for its bright blue flowers which are added to salads and drinks such as Pimms.

liquid and are a welcome addition to many vegetable dishes, including artichokes, and to milk puddings. Bay leaf is an essential constituent of *bouquet garni*. The leaves should always be removed before liquidizing or sieving any dish as the minute fragments may be harmful. (see p. 39)

Borage

Borago officinalis L.   Boraginaceae
A traditional plant of herb gardens, borage is grown not so much for its possibly underrated culinary value as for its brilliant blue flowers and its former repute; thus herbalist John Gerard wrote in 1597 that it was 'used everywhere for the comfort of the hart, for

the driving away of sorrowe, and increasing the joie of the mind' and 'the leaves and flowers of Borage put into wine, maketh men and women glad and merrie and driveth away all sadnesse, dulnesse and melancholie', although its efficacy here may have depended more upon the wine than the herb!

Borage is an annual between 1½ and 2½ feet (45 to 75 cm) high with hairy leaves and clusters of drooping bright blue five-petalled starry flowers about 1 inch (2.5 cm) across with a black cone of stamens in the middle. A native of southern Europe it has become naturalised in the warmer parts of western Europe; it seeds freely and maintains itself by self-sown seedlings on light soil. On heavy soil however, it is necessary to harvest the seed in early autumn and store it in a dry place, and sow in a sunny position from March to July. Seed can be sown from March to July in a sunny position. Both leaves and flowers are sometimes placed in alcoholic drinks such as claret or Pimms; they can also be chopped and added to salads for their cucumber flavour. (see p. 34)

Caraway
Carum carvi L.   Umbelliferae (Apiaceae)

Caraway is a biennial or perennial branched plant occurring widely in Europe, about 2 feet (60 cm) high, the leaves being pinnately divided into very narrow segments and the small flowers whitish or pink. It is grown commercially for its aromatic fruits, which are used in cakes, rye bread, some cheeses, pickles, soups and meat and fish dishes, but the young leaves and stems can be added to salads.

Those who wish to grow their own caraway seed should sow it in May in a sunny well-drained border and thin seedlings to 4 to 6 inches (10–15 cm) apart. The seed will ripen in July and August the following year; as soon as the main umbels are ripe, the plants are cut at ground level and hung upside down in small bunches over a cloth in a well-ventilated shed for the flowerheads to ripen. Caraway sets seed very freely and self sown seedlings will be troublesome if the seed is not harvested.

Chervil
Anthriscus cerefolium (L.) Hoffmann   Umbelliferae (Apiaceae)

Chervil is a fragile quick-growing hardy annual up to 2 feet (60 cm) high with a much divided leaf and small white flowers, apparently native in eastern central Europe, southern and eastern Europe, but naturalised in many countries. Sowings made in August and September in a sunny open border will provide plants for use in winter. Sowings for summer use should be made from

February to April on a border in half shade on moist soil, for in hot dry weather it will quickly run to seed. Seed is sown where the plants are to mature as they cannot be successfully transplanted. When the leaves are being gathered, most flower stems should be cut away, allowing only a few scattered plants to go to seed and provide a self-grown crop. Seed remains viable for only a short time. If a shady corner of the garden is chosen for chervil re-seeding will be continuous.

Chervil has a distinct sweet aniseed aroma and flavour, which is most pronounced in the fresh green state. It is an important ingredient of *fines herbes*. Its flavour being evanescent, it is added to soups and other dishes only shortly before serving. As a garnish to *hors d'oeuvres* and salads it should likewise be added only at the last moment, since it wilts rapidly.

Chinese Chives
Allium tuberosum Rottler ex Sprengel   Amaryllidaceae (or Alliaceae)

Chinese chives is a convenient English name for a species cultivated for at least two thousand years in China, which, although not closely related to chives (*A. schoenoprasum*), has similar culinary uses; a Chinese name Kui Ts'ai (Kau Ts'oi) is sometimes also rendered as Cuchay.

It forms dense clumps of narrow bulbs covered with a brown net-like tunic, arising from tough rhizomatous-like growth, and ascending flat (not tubular and cylindric) leaves to 15 inches (40 cm) long, $\frac{3}{10}$ inch (8 mm) wide. The flower-stems are angular and up to $1\frac{1}{2}$ feet (45 cm) high, carrying a many-flowered umbel of pleasing white fragrant starry flowers. The species has a wide range in eastern Asia, along the Himalaya and across China to Japan, but in parts of this area it may be an escape from cultivation. It is very easy to grow in a sunny place. The flower-heads should be cut off after flowering as they produce such abundant seed that self-sown seedlings can be a nuisance. The clumps can be divided in spring. The leaves can be used like those of chives and the flowers likewise sprinkled in salads.

Chives
Allium schoenoprasum L.   Amaryllidaceae (or Alliaceae)

Chives belongs to the same genus as garlic, leek and onion but has a much milder flavour and a different habit of growth. It forms dense tufts of narrow grassy tubular leaves in the usual cultivated form up to 10 inches (25 cm) high, with scarcely taller flower-stems ending in close heads of rose-purple flowers. The species

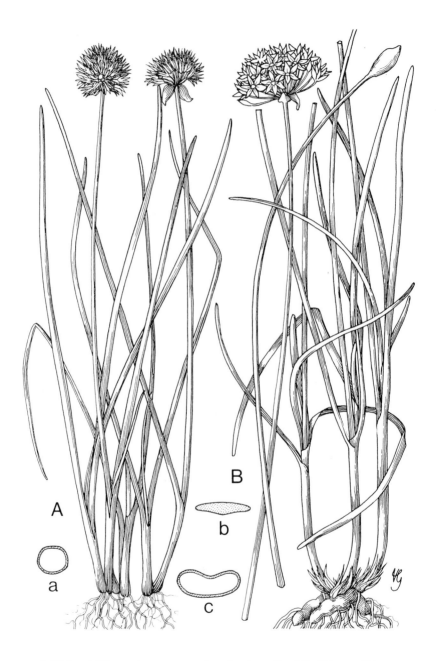

A. Chives (*Allium schoenoprasum*). a, Section of leaf. B. Chinese Chives (*A. tuberosum*). b, Section of leaf. C. Every-ready Onion (*A. cepa* 'Perutile') section of leaf.

has an extraordinarily wide range all round the northern hemisphere and exists in a diversity of forms, the largest of which may be up to 2 feet (60 cm) high. Although chives will grow in most soils, the most satisfactory is a moist friable soil rich in humus with full sun; it should be kept well-watered. Young leaves being the most palatable, they are cut to within a inch or two of the ground during the growing season; hence several clumps are necessary even for a small household in order to provide a succession of new growth in rotation. The bulbs, which are very narrow, almost pencil-like, increase rapidly; the clumps become overcrowded in the course of three or four years and should be lifted and divided in either spring or autumn. The chopped leaves can be sprinkled over most savoury dishes, added to salads and soups and incorporated in omelettes and even butter. Surplus bulbs can be pickled in white wine vinegar for winter use.

Chives makes a pleasant and useful edging for a herb garden.

A narrow-leaved perennial variant of the ordinary onion known as the Ever-Ready onion or *Allium cepa* 'Perutile' is like chives in forming dense tufts and providing onion-flavoured foliage for seasoning but is much more robust and has a stronger flavour; the bulb-coats are reddish and the leaves, most of which remain green all winter, are flattened or shallowly grooved on one side, not completely round in section like those of chives. It increases rapidly in good soil and can be divided and replanted at almost any time. It rarely flowers.

Costmary

Balsamita major Desf.   Compositae (Asteraceae)

Costmary, in the United States sometimes known as mint-geranium and in parts of England as alecost, French sage and goose-tongue, has likewise a diversity of botanical names reflecting difficulty about the right genus in which to classify it: *Tanacetum balsamita* L., *Chrysanthemum balsamita* (L) L., *Balsamita vulgaris* Willd., *Pyrethrum balsamita* (L) Willd. It is a herbaceous perennial of easy cultivation, $1\frac{1}{2}$ to 4 feet (45 to 120 cm) high, with branched stems ending in clusters of small yellow-flowered heads usually rayless but sometimes with a few white rays of no decorative value. Its virtue is in its greyish green finely toothed leaves, the lower of which are stalkless and more ovate, possessing a lightly bitter mint flavour and a pleasant scent and often available in winter when mints have died down completely. They can be used in mint sauce and soups and in stuffing. Before the introduction of the hop plant it was used to flavour beer, hence its common name of Alecost.

A. Rosemary (*Rosmarinus officinalis*). B. Costmary (*Balsamita major*) with a portion of the inflorescence (see pp. 51 and 23).

It is a native of Asia Minor, the Caucasus and Iran but has become naturalised in southern Europe. It grows readily in a good soil retentive of moisture and in a sunny position. As it is a rapid grower it needs dividing and replanting every 3 or 4 years. This can be done in spring or autumn.

Dill

Anethum graveolens L.   Umbelliferae (Apiaceae)

Dill is a hardy aromatic annual 1 to 2½ feet (30 to 70 cm) high, rather like a seedling fennel, with much divided threadlike bluish green leaves and small deep yellow flowers in flat or saucer-shaped umbels up to 8 inches (20 cm) across. It is a native of southern Europe and western Asia. The elliptical three-ribbed dark brown 'seeds' have a pale wing around them. Gripe water or dill water for babies is made from these 'seeds' which are more strongly aromatic than the leaves; they can be used whole or ground and added to salads or fish. The leaves finely chopped add a distinctive taste to fish.

Seed is sown where the crop is to grow and the seedlings thinned to 9 or 12 inches (23 to 30 cm) apart. April sowing is

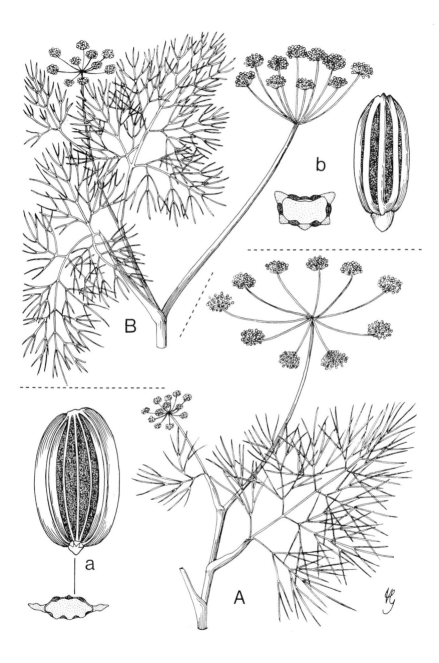

A. Dill (*Anethum graveolens*); a, side view and section of half-fruit.
B. Fennel (*Foeniculum vulgare*); b, side view and section of half-fruit.

recommended for a seed crop, but for a continuous supply of young leaves successive sowings can be made from April to late June. Clean ground or persistent weeding is essential, so that the very small seedlings do not have to compete with more vigorous weeds. A sunny well-drained sheltered border where they will suffer neither from draught or strong winds is best. The 'seeds' scatter as soon as ripe; hence the plants are pulled up or cut at ground level as the main flowerheads become brown; they are then tied in bunches and hung in a sunny airy place over a cloth. Leaves to be dried for winter use should be cut while still young, spread in a thin layer and dried in a temperature not above 100°F (38°C).

Fennel

Foeniculum vulgare Miller　　　　　　　　Umbelliferae (Apiaceae)

Fennel is a vigorous but graceful hardy perennial native to southern Europe and occurring wild, though probably naturalised, in many parts of Europe including Britain, particularly in coastal districts. The fennel grown as a garden plant would appear to be a selected form. It is milder and more attractive in flavour and has finer hair-like leaf growth. It grows up to 5 feet (1.5 m), the smooth glossy erect stems bearing widely spaced leaves several times pinnately divided into numerous thread-like segments with a bluish tinge. The yellow flowers are borne in flat umbels up to 6 inches (15 cm) across; the fruits, which are ribbed but not winged, have a pleasant flavour and can be used whole in savoury dishes and sprinkled on fruit, bread, cakes and biscuits. Fennel will grow in a variety of conditions but gives best results when given a sunny place on a deep well-drained moisture-retaining soil. Plants of fennel age rapidly and only young growth is suitable for culinary use. This can be obtained by several methods, i.e. by cutting mature shoots to the ground during the growing season, by frequent division of plants in winter, or by annual or biennial sowing or saving a few of the self sown seedlings which are freely produced. The ornamental bronze leaved form is equally valuable as a herb plant.

Fennel has a pleasing sweet aniseed flavour and when chopped can be added to fish, poultry, salads and vegetables, especially peas, beans, cabbage and cauliflower; it is sometimes sprinkled on potatoes instead of parsley, but its most effective use is probably with grilled herrings or mackerel or in a sauce to be served with these fish.

Florence fennel or finocchio is a variant of sweet fennel with a bulb-like structure formed by the leaf bases which is served either raw in a salad or cooked as a vegetable, like celery, braised or with a rich sauce. It has long been popular in France and Italy and is becoming increasingly popular in England. Another variant is carosella, which has fleshy leaf and flower stems and is served in the same way. The young foliage of either of these plants can be used as a herb and is milder in flavour than sweet fennel.

Finocchio and carosella are less easy to grow successfully and tend to run to seed prematurely, but if seed sowing is delayed until June the warmer weather encourages the succulent growth needed for the kitchen. Both plants need a light, well drained soil rich in humus and copious supplies of water in dry periods. They have to be raised from seed each year. Finocchio should be sown in drills in mid June 18 inches, (45 cm) apart and thinned to 9 inches (22 cm). When the leaf bases are about $1\frac{1}{2}$ inches (4 cm) in diameter at the widest point they must be earthed up. Keep the crop free of weeds. In three or four weeks they should be ready for use. Good samples of home grown Finocchio are occasionally to be seen in village shops.

Garlic

Allium sativum L.   Amaryllidaceae (or Alliaceae)

Wandering in the wilderness of Sinai in the thirteenth century B.C., the Israelites pined for the garlic, onions and leeks they had relished in Egypt but, as garlic and onions have their closest relatives, probably the wild species from which they were domesticated, in central Asia, their first cultivation must go much further back in time than that; the pungency of wild alliums often causes native peoples to gather them for flavouring.

Garlic is a bulbous plant 1 to 3 feet (30 to 90 cm) tall with several flat (not hollow) leaves sheathing the lower part of the stem, which ends sometimes in a cluster of bulbils and a few flowers. The large bulb which forms below ground is usually entire when harvested but when fully ripened will split into bulblets, called cloves, enclosed within a pale brownish or yellowish papery covering. These bulblets are used both for flavouring and planting. This is one of the easiest herbs to grow and needs the minimum of attention. In southern England planting can take place out of doors in October or November, elsewhere it may be wiser to delay it until early March. A well worked fertile soil in a sunny position is necessary to obtain good bulbs. Select the larger bulblets (cloves) from the previous year's crop, planting them in rows 12 inches (30 cm) apart, 8 inches (20 cm) apart in the row and 2 inches (5 cm) deep. The only care required is to keep the plants free of weeds and well watered in dry weather. In August, when the leaves begin to yellow the bulbs are lifted and left in the sun until the foliage is completely dry; the tops are then shortened to a few inches. On lifting the bulbs may appear to be entire, but as they become thoroughly dry the cloves will be visible through the transparent skin. If the bulbs are not lifted until all the foliage is yellow the outer skins may split and the bulblets scatter. For storage the ripened bulbs should not be bunched but tied into strings, as onions. Store in a dry, warm place. A low storage temperature and damp often encourage premature growth, thus shortening the useful season of the crop.

Garlic is cultivated commercially on a large scale in southern and eastern Europe, notably Spain and Romania, and also in Egypt, California, Mexico and Brazil.

The common prejudice against garlic is due largely to its over-use. It is a valuable seasoning containing the vitamins A, B and C and sulphur and used in small amounts enhances the flavour of a dish. The cloves should be cut into slivers and inserted into a joint of meat or poultry for roasting, or pounded or pressed and added to sauces, casseroles etc. A little garlic can be added to salad dressing, or a very mild flavour obtained by rubbing a clove round the inside of a casserole or salad bowl.

Used moderately, garlic improves the flavour of many dishes; eaten immoderately it makes the breath obnoxious or even nauseating! According to Boulestin and Hill, 'Garlic was highly valued in the Middle Ages for its power of keeping vampires at a distance and, if consumed in liberal quantities, it will be found equally efficacious today'. They note, however, that in many cases the taste of garlic is undetectable, but the small quantity employed is necessary to the final harmonious whole.

There are many local variants of garlic.

Horseradish
Armoracia rusticana Gaert.
Meyer & Scherb.   Cruciferae (Brassicaceae)
Horseradish sauce is a condiment which the Romans would have relished with their beef but did not have. A native of south-eastern Europe, horseradish, often known as *Cochlearia armoracia* L., seems not to have come into culinary use until the late Middle Ages in central Europe, passing thence to Britain, where it is now widely naturalised as an escape from cultivation, despite its reluctance to set seed here. The stout fleshy rootstocks and long roots are very tenacious of life and once established they become difficult to eradicate, since small pieces of root left in the soil can produce new plants. It makes thick tufts of large erect leaves up to about 2 feet (60 cm) high, the first ones deeply cut and quite unlike the later ones which are more or less oblong with a wavy edge, in general appearance like those of dock (*Rumex*) and it sends up

much branched flowering stems to 4 feet (1.2 m) high with small white flowers in summer.

Horseradish is very easy to grow but to get really good roots the soil, preferably a moist, rich but light one, should be dug to a depth of 2 feet (60 cm) at least and enriched with plenty of manure; the usual recommended procedure for commercial growing is to dig a trench 2 feet (60 cm) or more deep, put about 1¼ feet (35 cm) of the top soil in this, then a layer of manure dug into that. For large, succulent roots the plants should be kept well watered. Thick side roots cut from the harvested crop and trimmed to about 6 inches (15 cm) long, are then planted with a dibber a foot apart in February or March, and the sub-soil put on top to a thickness of 4 inches (10 cm). A heavier crop will be obtained if the plants are left undisturbed until the second autumn. When harvesting the bed must be cleared of all roots. The main roots are stored in moist sand until required for use and thongs for the next year's crop prepared from the thickest of the side shoots. These also must be stored in sand until needed for planting in the spring. (see p. 38)

Lemon Balm

Melissa officinalis L.   Labiatae (Lamiaceae)

A hardy perennial herb, lemon balm (also known as bee balm) merits an unimportant place in the garden for the strong lemon fragrance, which the leaves give out when handled or crushed, rather than for culinary value; it makes a bushy plant up to 2½ feet (70 cm) high, the much-branched stems bearing numerous paired stalked wrinkled deeply toothed ovate leaves to 3½ inches (9 cm) long, 2½ inches (6 cm) broad, with clusters of small narrow white flowers in the axils of the upper leaves. The rootstock is compact but easily divided in spring or autumn and seed is so freely produced that self-sown seedlings may become a nuisance. Balm will grow in almost any soil and any position; thanks to this accommodating disposition it has become widely naturalised in northern Europe although native to southern Europe. Its flavour is not as strong as its scent, but the chopped leaves can be added to fruit salad, custards, soups etc. A refreshing drink can be made by infusing the fresh or dried leaves in boiling water for up to five minutes.

The Latin name *Melissa* is associated with the ancient Greek usage of the plant as a bee plant; many beekeepers plant lemon balm in the vicinity of their hives.

Lemon Verbena

Aloysia triphylla (L'Hérit.) Britton   Verbenaceae

Lemon verbena, also known as *Aloysia citriodora* Ortega and

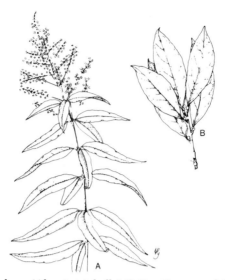

A. Lemon verbena (*Aloysia triphylla*). B. Bay (*Laurus nobilis*) (see p. 18).

Lippia citriodora (Ort.) Kunth, is a shrubby plant very liable to damage in a severe winter; hence it both needs and merits a warm sheltered place in well-drained unmanured soil at the foot of a south-facing wall, where it may reach a height of 10 feet (3 m). The lanceolate leaves, up to 3 inches (8 cm) long, are borne three or four together and have a strong persistent aromatic lemon smell and flavour. The small lilac or white flowers in small panicles at the ends of the shoots in late summer and autumn are not particularly attractive. It comes from Chile and Argentina and was not introduced into England until the late eighteenth century. In places with severe winter conditions it can be grown in a tub or large pot, stood outside in the summer and taken into a frost-free house for the winter. It is easily propagated by soft or ripe woody cuttings.

The leaves of lemon verbena have a much stronger and more lasting flavour than those of lemon balm and can be used in any foods where a lemon flavour is needed. A fragrant sedative tea can be made from a teaspoonful of crushed or dry leaves per cup of boiling water. Dried leaves put among linen or added to pot pourri keep their fragrance for years. (see p. 35)

Lovage
Levisticum officinale Koch   Umbelliferae (Apiaceae)
Lovage is a large strong-growing tall perennial sometimes up to 8 feet (2.5 m). Its foliage is somewhat like that of a vigorous celery plant, with pinnately divided leaves having broad deeply lobed dark green and glossy leaflets. The small yellowish green flowers

in umbels nearly 6 inches (15 cm) across are followed by large ovoid-oblong brown fruits, which like all other parts of the plant can be used for flavouring. The young shoots as they emerge from the soil in early spring are an attractive deep bronze colour. Although now widespread in Europe, it may be really an ancient introduction from the Middle East. Occasionally it may be heavily attacked by leaf mining fly, possibly the celery fly. This can be controlled to a certain extent by cutting all the affected shoots to the ground and burning them. These will soon be replaced by new growth which, in any case, is what is needed in the kitchen.

Lovage has a strong yeasty aroma and taste and, used in small quantities, enriches the flavour of savoury dishes. The young leaves and stalks cut into 2-inch (5 cm) lengths can be added to

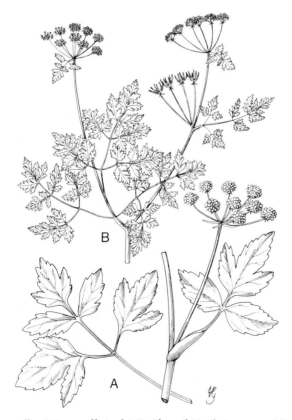

A. Lovage (*Levisticum officinale*). B. Chervil (*Anthriscus cerefolium*) (see p. 20).

soups, casseroles and meat and poultry cooked in liqluid. A handful of fresh crushed leaves rubbed on to meats before roasting
improves the flavour. In some Mediterranean countries the
crushed seed is used to spice bread, cakes and biscuits. The leaf-
stalks can be handled like angelica.

Lovage is easily raised from seed, which is best sown as soon as
ripe. The seedlings are transplanted in autumn or spring, spaced
2 feet (60 cm) apart. It is generally propagated by division, the
fleshy roots being cut into pieces in early spring as the new
growth breaks through the soil, each piece having a shoot or bud.
It grows well on most soils, but does best on deep moist well-
worked loam.

Marjoram

Origanum vulgare L. (Wild marjoram)	Labiatae (Lamiaceae)
Origanum majorana L. (Sweet marjoram)	
Origanum onites L. (Pot marjoram)	

Wild marjoram or oregano (*O. vulgare*) has a wide distribution in
Europe, including the British Isles, where it may be very
abundant on chalk downs and hedge-banks. It is an erect
perennial with a woody rhizomatous rootstock, from which arise
annual leafy stems, to $2\frac{1}{2}$ feet (70 cm) high, branched in the upper
part with ovate leaves about 1 inch (2.5 cm) long, usually hairy on
both sides, and with terminal clusters of small magenta-pink
flowers surrounded by purple-tipped bracts. The calyx has 5
equal teeth, which distinguishes it from both the sweet marjoram
(sometimes called *Majorana hortensis* Moench) and pot marjoram
(sometimes called *Majorana onites* (L.) Benth.) with the calyx split
down the back.

Origanum vulgare is a very variable species and the British
plants are not as strongly fragrant as those growing on the hot
mountain slopes of southern Europe. The popular name of these
latter plants is oregano. Deep coloured and also pure white forms
are sometimes grown as border plants. A small form with
glabrous leaves and pale pink flowers is more commonly grown
in herb collections. There is also a form with yellow leaves,
'Aureum'. Wild marjoram needs a well-drained calcareous soil in
full sun; it is propagated by division in spring or autumn and is
easily raised from seed. Owing to the strong flavour of the
imported oregano this should be used in small quantities, as it is
in the Italian dish *pizza*, to which the dried leaves are added.
Leaves for drying are collected in July and August.

The name 'Oregano' is applied in Mexico to the more pungent
Lippia graveolens Kunth (Verbenaceae).

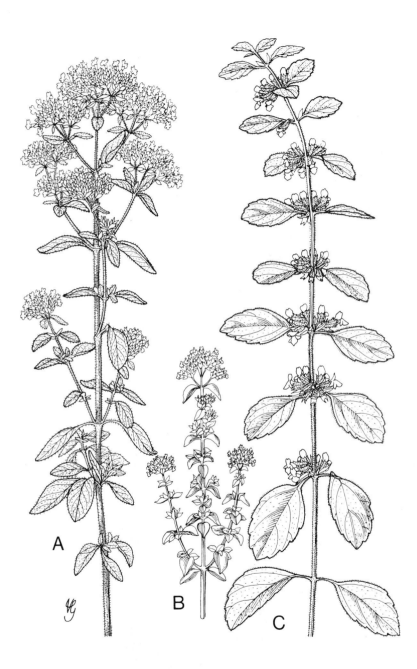

A. Wild Marjoram (*Origanum vulgare*). B. Pot Marjoram (*Origanum onites*). C. Lemon Balm (*Melissa officinalis*).

Above: Borage, *Borago officinalis*, showing the brilliant blue flowers for which it is esteemed (see pp. 19–20).
Below: Chives, *Allium schoenoprasum*, showing flower buds. The leaves can be chopped and sprinkled over most savoury dishes and the bulbs may be pickled (see pp. 21–23).

Above: The leaves of Lemon verbena, *Aloysia triphylla*, have a strong aromatic lemon scent and flavour. These can be used to make fragrant teas, to flavour puddings, and may be dried for use in pot pourri (see p.30). Below: Angelica, *Angelica archangelica*, an attractive and useful plant, whose stems and young leaf stalks may be candied (see p. 16).

Sweet, annual or knotted marjoram (*O. majorana*), a native of southern Europe, North Africa and western Asia, is not hardy in Britain and must be grown here as a half-hardy annual. It forms a small upright bush 1 foot (30 cm) tall or more with broadly elliptic or obovate blunt leaves, usually grey and minutely hairy. The small pale lilac, pink or white flowers are enveloped in rounded leafy bracts and borne in globose to oblong heads, forming a narrow inflorescence. Seed rarely ripens in England. A sowing can be made in open ground in late May, but seed is usually sown in a cold frame in March and the small plants transferred to their final quarters in mid or late May, allowing 6 to 10 inches (15 to 25 cm) between them. As the seed is very fine, it is usually mixed with sand or dry soil to get even distribution; it is often slow to germinate. A winter supply can be obtained by potting plants from the open ground in sandy soil in late summer and housing in a frost-free greenhouse.

Sweet marjoram has a much milder and more pleasant flavour than wild marjoram and thus is used in greater quantity, notably in meat dishes. (see p. 38)

Pot marjoram (*O. onites*) is a dwarf shrub with erect densely hairy stems up to 2 feet (60 cm) high; the leaves are smaller than those of wild marjoram, rounded or cordate at base, the lower ones stalked, the upper ones sessile. The pale pink or white flowers are borne in ovoid or oblong heads, forming an inflorescence much denser than that of wild marjoram. A native of the eastern Mediterranean region, it needs a warm light well-drained soil with plenty of humus in a sheltered position. It is readily propagated by division or by seed. The basal leaves of this marjoram form attractive mats of green foliage throughout most winters.

Mints

Mentha   Labiatae (Lamiaceae)

M. × gentilis L. (Ginger mint)

M. × *gentilis* 'Variegata' (Variegated ginger mint)

M. *longifolia* (L.) Hudson (Horse mint)

M. × *piperita* L. nm. *officinalis* Sole (White peppermint)

M. × *piperita* L. nm. *piperita* (Black peppermint)

M. × *piperita* L. 'Crispa' (Curly mint)

M. × *piperita* L. nm. *citrata* (Ehrhart) Briquet (Eau de Cologne mint)

M. *pulegium* L. (Pennyroyal)

M. *spicata* L. (Spearmint)

M. *suaveolens* Ehrhart (Round-leaved mint)

M. suaveolens 'Variegata' (Pineapple mint)

M. × *villosa* nm. *alopecuroides* (Hull) Briquet (Bowles mint)

M. × *villosonervata* Opiz (Horse mint)

Mints are among the oldest of European herbs, their culinary use probably going back to neolithic times in southern Europe. The mint grown and used by the Romans 2000 years ago was apparently water mint (*M. aquatica* L.). The Greek name *minthe* and the Latin *menta* are considered to have been taken from a much older and long vanished language spoken in the Mediterranean region before the coming of the ancestors of the Ancient Greek and Latin peoples into Greece and Italy between 3000 and 4000 years ago.

As a group the mints are very difficult to understand and classify, the species being very variable, their hybrids both many and widespread and the literature about them extensive but scattered and sometimes contradictory; not surprisingly the names given to plants of this confusing assemblage have themselves become confused in their application. The names accepted here are those used by R. M. Harley in *Flora Europaea* 3: 183–186 (1972).

The mint most commonly grown for culinary purposes is spearmint, *M. spicata*, but other kinds have their own special virtues, possessing between them a diversity of fresh clean scents and flavours, which have led to their use in mint sauce, mint jelly, mint tea, chocolate, menthol, toothpaste, chewing gum and liqueurs. They are mostly vigorous herbaceous perennials with invasive long underground runners which make them bad neighbours for other herbs. Hence they should be given a bed of their own. When several kinds of mint are grown together in a confined area, their spread should be restricted by embedding metal strips to a depth of 6 inches (15 cm) or so in the soil around them or putting them in bottomless containers; otherwise the more robust growers will oust their weaker brethren. They grow wild in damp or wet places and rarely thrive in dry ones. The use of peppermint and spearmint for flavouring toothpaste, chewing gum etc. has led to their commercial large-scale cultivation, particularly in the U.S.A.

A moist rich soil in half-shade suits mints best. A bed for them should be well dug and enriched with well-decayed manure or compost worked into the surface. Rooted pieces of the runners are planted about 2 inches deep (5 cm), 6 to 9 inches apart (15 to 23 cm), in rows 9 to 12 inches apart (23 to 30 cm), in February or March. At the end of a season's growth, the bed is cleared of shoots, a common method to combat mint rust being to pack dry straw on the bed among the dead or dying stalks and set light to it

Above: Horseradish, *Armoracia rusticana*, is well known for its roots which are used to make that essential accompaniment to roast beef! Horseradish prefers a moist, rich but light soil (see p. 28).

Below: The flowers of sweet marjoram, *Origanum marjorana*, a herb grown in Britain as a half-hardy annual (see p. 36).

Above: Clipped specimens of bay (*Laurus nobilis*) can make attractive formal plants for tubs (see p. 18).

Below: There are several forms of Rosemary, *Rosmarinus officinalis*, in cultivation in Britain. As the illustration on page 1 shows, this shrub thrives in full sun (see p. 51).

Mentha × *gentilis* 'Variegata', variegated ginger mint.

in the autumn; it can then be top dressed with decayed manure. As mints exhaust the soil, they should be replanted every 2 or 3 years, the soil being dug over and manured, or a new bed made on a fresh site.

Mints can be badly affected by mint rust caused by the fungus *Puccinia menthae*; this does not perennate inside the underground parts but infects the young growing shoots in spring from spores (teleutospores) formed on the leaves of infected plants the previous autumn and dropped into the soil; hence the practice of burning over a bed with straw in late autumn and winter. The first signs are thickened shoots in spring on which appear small orange cups; such shoots should be pulled up at once and burnt as the spores from them will infect the leaves of other plants, producing orange or rusty patches of spores (aecidiospores). Runners from an infected area should be washed completely free of soil before being planted elsewhere, and are best disinfected first by immersing them in hot water kept at 105° to 115°F (41–46°C) for 10 minutes, then washing them in cold water.

Since mints tend to be confused and are hard to sort out, the following series of contrasting statements is intended as a guide to the main kinds of culinary mints. Thus if you have a very hairy robust mint with boldly variegated leaves but have lost the label, you can find out its name by checking it against these statements. First, it is not pennyroyal, because its leaves are more than 1 inch long. The leaves being variegated, it evidently belongs to the group with variegated leaves and, because they are very hairy, it must be pineapple mint.

KEY TO CULINARY MINTS

1. Leaves not more than 1 in. (2.5 cm) long, ½ in. (14 mm) broad   ...   ...
                                                                    Pennyroyal (*M. pulegium*)
1. Leaves some or all more than 1 in. (2.5 cm) long, ½ in. (1.3 cm) broad   ...   2
  2. Leaves abnormal, i.e. variegated or crisped (the margin irregularly waved,
     twisted or curled)   3
    3. Leaves variegated   4
      4. Stems very hairy. Leaves irregularly whitish-variegated   ...   ...
                                              Pineapple mint (*M. suaveolens* 'Variegata')
      4. Stems almost hairless or sparsely hairy. Leaves golden-variegated along
         the veins ...   .
                                    Variegated Ginger mint (*M.* × *gentilis* 'Variegata')
    3. Leaves crisped   5
      5. Flower-clusters (whorls) in axils of leaves, the terminal pair without
         flowers ...   .   *M.* × gentilis 'Crispa'
      5. Flower-clusters forming a terminal spike or head   6
        6. Leaves about as long as broad   ...   ...   *M.* × *piperita* 'Crispa'
        6. Leaves much longer than broad   7
          7. Leaves almost hairless   ...   .   *M. spicata* 'Crispa'
          7. Leaves very hairy ...   .   *M.* × *longifolia* 'Crispa'
  2. Leaves normal, not variegated or crisped   8
      8. Leaves all stalkless or else some with stalk not more than ⅛ in.
         (4 mm) long   9
        9. Leaves not much longer than broad (length : breadth = about 6
           : 4 or 5), densely hairy with long hairs   10
          10. Leaves sharply toothed, to 2½ in. (6.5 cm) broad. Stamens
              not longer than corolla   ...   .
                                        Bowles mint (*M.* × *villosa alopecuroides*)
          10. Leaves mostly with rounded shallow teeth, rarely more
              than 1½ in. (4 cm) broad. Stamens longer than corolla
                                              Round-leaved mint (*M. suaveolens*)
        9. Leaves much longer than broad (often about 3 times as long
           as broad), almost hairless or with close very short hairs   11
          11. Leaves almost hairless, bright green   ...   .
                                              Spearmint (*M. spicata*)
          11. Leaves covered with short hairs, greyish   ...   ...
                                  Horse mint (*M. longifolia*, *M.* × *villosonervata*)
      8. Leaves stalked, the stalk more than ⅛ in. (4 mm) long   ...   12
        12. Flower-clusters (whorls) in axils of leaves or of leafy
            bracts up the stem but the terminal pair without flowers
                                              Ginger mint (*M.* × *gentilis*)
        12. Flower-clusters at ends of shoots forming a terminal
            head or spike   13
          13. Leaf-blade lanceolate, about 3 times as long as broad
                                  White peppermint (*M.* × *piperita officinalis*)
          13. Leaf-blade ovate, about 2 or 1½ times as long as broad
                14
            14. Leaf-blade often more than 2 in. (5 cm) long, with
                length : breadth = about 4 or 3 : 2. Peppermint smell
                                  Black Peppermint (*M.* × *piperita piperita*)
            14. Leaf-blade rarely more than 2 in. (5 cm) long, with
                length : breadth = about 3 : 2. Lemony smell   ...
                                  Eau de Cologne mint (*M.* × *piperita citrata*)

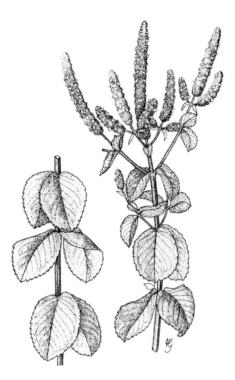

Bowles mint (*Mentha* × *villosa alopecurioides*).

Bowles mint (*M.* × *villosa* nm. *alopecuroides*), sometimes known as the round-leaved fox-tail mint, woolly mint or *M. rotundifolia* 'Bowles's Variety', is considered to be a hybrid of *M. spicata* and *M. suaveolens*. It takes its common name from Edward Augustus Bowles (1865–1954) who used to recommend it for making the best mint sauce. A very rampant grower, ranging from 2 to 4 feet (60 to 120 cm) according to conditions, it does better on dry soils than most mints. The large woolly sessile leaves are almost round and up to 3 inches (7.5 cm) long. The lilac flowers are borne in long dense terminal spikes which can be used in flower arrangements.

Although highly esteemed for private use Bowles mint has no commercial value because it wilts rapidly when picked. The feltiness of the leaves is not noticeable when they are finely chopped for mint sauce; their rich minty flavour goes well with new potatoes and fresh green peas. It is not so susceptible to mint rust as spearmint.

Mentha spicata 'Crispa', one of several different curly mints that have waved and twisted leaves.

Curly mint is a general name given to mints with the leaves variously waved, twisted and curled and sometimes deeply toothed. Such 'Crispa' forms arise as variants in most species and hybrids of *Mentha* when raised on a large scale. The one recorded longest was named *M. crispa* by Linnaeus in 1753 and has leaves about as broad as long and hairy below towards the base. It is now considered to be derived from the crossing of *Mentha aquatica* and *M. spicata* and hence is placed under *M. × piperita*. There are also 'Crispa' forms of *M. × gentilis*, *M. longifolia* and of *M. spicata*.

Eau de Cologne mint (*M. × piperita* nm. *citrata*), also known as lemon mint, bergamot mint, orange mint, *M. piperita* var. *citriodora*. *M. × piperita citrata* is considered to be a hybrid of *M. aquatica* and *M. spicata*, thus having the same parents as peppermint, from which it differs in scent. It is a hairless plant with stems up to 20 inches (50 cm) high, with distinctly stalked thin smooth leaves and small terminal heads of purplish flowers. It spreads invasively by purple runners both above and below ground. Grown in a sunny place, where it will develop to the full its characteristic scented oil reminiscent of eau de cologne, the whole plant acquires a marked purplish tinge: grown in shade it is greener and has a faint coppery flush. Those who like unusual flavours should try a vinegar sauce made from this mint with a rich dish such as roast pork. A bunch of eau de cologne mint in an airing cupboard will pleasantly scent linen and it is a valuable addition to pot pourri. As stated by Claire Loewenfeld, 'leaves infused in boiling water, sweetened with honey, provide an excellent summer drink hot or cold'. Its scent is better than its flavour.

Ginger mint (M. × gentilis), also called slender mint and Scotch mint, is derived from the crossing of the corn mint (M. arvensis) and Spearmint (M. spicata) and is pungently scented much as the latter. It grows about 1 to 2 feet high (30 to 60 cm) and has branched stems with numerous short-stalked small leaves pointed at both ends and mostly less than 2 inches (5 cm) long, in the axils of which are borne the clusters of lilac flowers; the shoots end in leaves or bracts, not in a terminal head or spike of flowers. In the form 'Variegata' the stripes of yellow, which contrast with the green of the rest of the leaf, run along the midrib and the main side veins.

A. Variegated ginger mint (Mentha × gentilis 'Variegata'). B. Pennyroyal (M. pulegium).

Horse mint (M. *longifolia*), also known as long-leaved mint and M. *sylvestris*, is a very hairy species, of more value in the garden for its grey foliage than its somewhat musty scent. It grows about 1½ to 3 feet (45 to 90 cm) high and has dense terminal spikes of lilac or white flowers. Although in cultivation typical spearmint (M. *spicata*) with its hairless leaves can be easily distinguished from typical horse mint, there exist wild intermediate forms. Spearmint is considered to have originated from this species by hybridization with round-leaved mint (A. *suaveolens*) followed by doubling of its chromosomes. Some plants cultivated under this name probably belong to the hybrid group called M. × *villosonervata*.

Pennyroyal (M. *pulegium*, syn. *Pulegium vulgare*) stands apart from the other culinary mints by its small leaves and the calyx being hairy (instead of hairless) on the inside. It makes a creeping mat of light green shoots rooting freely in the soil and clothed with narrowly ovate or elliptic smooth light green leaves which are usually not more than ½ inch (14 mm) long and ¼ inch (7 mm) wide. During the summer it sends up erect branched flowering stems to a foot (30 cm) high with many well-separated clusters of mauve flowers.

Its completely robust habit and constitution make the prostrate form of pennyroyal a useful lawn plant for damp open places where grass is less successful; for such a lawn small tufts are planted 6 inches (15 cm) apart in spring or autumn; they quickly mat together and give off a delightful pepperminty smell when walked upon; a pennyroyal lawn is generally mown only twice a year.

Pennyroyal has a strong aroma and is used occasionally to flavour soups and stuffings; it may also be chopped and sprinkled lightly over buttered new potatoes.

Peppermint (M. × *piperita*) is of hybrid origin, its parents being water mint (M. *aquatica*) and spearmint (M. *spicata*), and although now widely cultivated and of great commercial importance, it seems to have been unrecorded until 1696 when John Ray coined the name 'peppermint' for it. All the world's peppermint crops are derived from these hybrids found in England in the seventeenth century.

Plants grow up to about 2 or 3 feet (60 to 90 cm) high and have stalked usually thinly hairy leaves. The lilac flowers are borne in an interrupted terminal spike or head.

There are two main forms of this, distinguished as the black peppermint (M. *piperita* nm. *piperita*, M. *piperita vulgaris* Sole) and the white peppermint (M. *piperita officinalis* Sole).

Black peppermint has deep purple erect stems to 2 feet (60 cm) and ovate or narrowly ovate leaf-blades up to about $2\frac{1}{2}$ inches (6 cm) long, $1\frac{1}{2}$ inches (4 cm) broad, with a purple tinge varying in intensity. This is the producer of peppermint oil. The commercial cultivation of peppermint began at Mitcham, Surrey in 1750.

White peppermint is less vigorous and less pungent than black peppermint. It has mostly lanceolate leaf-blades up to about 3 inches (7.5 cm) long, 1 inch (2.4 cm) broad, of a lighter green than those of black peppermint.

Peppermint tea is generally made from black peppermint, using a handful of fresh leaves or a teaspoonful of dried leaves on to which boiling water is poured and allowed to infuse for not more than 5 to 10 minutes before straining, otherwise unpleasant flavours may develop.

Black peppermint (*Mentha × piperita piperita*).

Above: Lovage (*Levisticum officinale*) has a strong aroma and both leaves and stalks are used in cooking (see p. 30).
Below: Pennyroyal, *Mentha pulegium*, showing the clusters of mauve flowers which are produced in summer (see p. 45).

Round-leaved mint (*M. suaveolens*) is a stout vigorous species often known as Apple Mint or *M. rotundifolia*, a name properly belonging to hybrids of this with *M. longifolia*. It has branching very hairy stems up to 2 feet (60 cm) high, with somewhat woolly wrinkled rather rounded sessile leaves, ending in dense spikes of lilac flowers. It combines the scent of ripe apples with a true mint flavour, but most people consider it inferior to Bowles mint for making mint sauce. In gardens it is usually represented by the form 'Variegata', sometimes called pineapple mint, with leaves partially splashed and blotched with creamy white or completely whitish, a decorative plant popular in flower arrangements. On heavy and compacted soils this mint may die out in wet winters; such soils should be made friable by the addition of coarse grit and humus.

Spearmint (*M. spicata*), also known as garden mint, lamb mint, pea mint and *M. viridis*, is the best known and most generally cultivated culinary mint but apparently nowhere occurs wild except as an escape from cultivation. It is believed to be derived from the crossing of horse mint (*M. longifolia*) and round-leaved mint (*M. suaveolens*); these have 24 chromosomes but it has 48. It grows about 1 to 1.4 feet (30 to 45 cm) high, with almost hairless stems and leaves, the latter being almost or quite stalkless, lanceolate and bright green. The lilac flowers are borne in long terminal spikes. The plants should be constantly cut back during the growing season to encourage fresh flowerless growth from the roots.

Spearmint, *Mentha spicata*, is the best known of all the mints (see above).

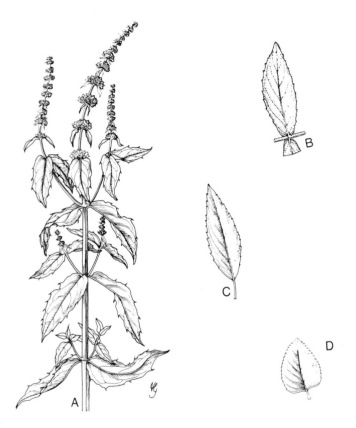

A. Spearmint (*Mentha spicata*). B. Horse Mint (*M. longifolia*). C. White peppermint (*M.* × *piperita officinalis*). D. Eau de Cologne mint (*M.* × *piperita citrata*).

Its cultivation has been set out above in the general note on mints. For window-box or pot cultivation this is the best mint but the soil must not be allowed to dry out. Sprigs are added to peas and new potatoes when cooking, but it is most commonly used in mint sauce with roast lamb. This can be made by chopping fresh young leaves very finely with white sugar and adding to malt vinegar or more elaborately by making a solution of white or brown sugar in boiling water, chopping the leaves very finely and mixing the leaves and sugar solution with wine vinegar, allowing the whole to stand for 2 or 3 hours before use.

Parsley

Petroselinum crispum (Miller) A. W. Hill   Umbelliferae (Apiaceae)
Parsley, probably native to southern Europe but so long cultivated
and naturalised as to make its original distribution uncertain, is
now the most commonly used of all herbs in Britain as a garnish
and a flavouring. The wild form has a plain but deeply segmented
leaf. The commonly grown form has curled and crisped segments
and thus cannot be mistaken for the poisonous and unpleasant-
smelling fools parsley (*Aethusa cynapium* L.)

Parsley is biennial; first-year plants produce finer and more
tender leaves than plants in their second year which are
preparing to flower and seed. Generally seed is sown where the
plants are to grow, perferably on a well-worked moisture-
retaining soil, although parsley will sometimes fail in conditions
which seem ideal and will thrive unexpectedly elsewhere. The
seeds take 5 to 8 weeks to germinate and should not be sown
before April but can then be sown up to August. In cold weather
germination can be hastened by pouring hot water on to the half-
covered drills. The germination period will be considerably
reduced if the soil is treated with hot water immediately before
sowing. The seedlings should be thinned until the remaining
plants stand 8 inches (20 cm) apart. Any check to growth such as
drought or injury to roots when transplanting may cause parsley
to run to seed; hence pricking out must be done carefully when
the plants are very small. Cutting out of the flowering stems in the
second year will lengthen the period of use. A winter supply of
leaves can be encouraged by covering plants with cloches or with
a frame.

Parsley is rich in vitamins and makes a valuable addition to any
savoury dish as well as being a very attractive garnish. There is a
greater concentration of flavour in the stems of parsley. For this
reason lengths of stem are always included in a *bouquet garni*.

Hamburg or turnip-rooted parsley (*P. crispum* 'Tuberosum') is
mainly grown for its fleshy roots which may be long and resemble
small parsnips or be short and resemble stump-rooted carrots.
The seed is sown in late March in deeply dug soil and the
seedlings are thinned to 12 to 15 inches (30 to 38 cm) apart; plenty
of moisture is essential and the crop should be grown in a shady
place. The roots are used in winter salads, in soups, and as a
vegetable; they are generally left in the ground until required. The
plants are hardier than the leafy moss-curled parsley and throughout the winter, even in the coldest weather, a few young fern-like
leaves can be found in the crowns of the fleshy roots; these will fill
the gap until the moss-curled forms are ready to pick in spring.

Hamburg parsley (*Petroselinum crispum* 'Tuberosum') is grown chiefly for its fleshy roots (see opposite).

Rosemary

Rosmarinus officinalis L.   Labiatae (Lamiaceae)
Rosemary is a densely leafy, evergreen shrub up to 6 feet (2 m) high with very numerous closely set firm linear leaves about ¾ to 1½ inches (2 to 4 cm) long, deep green above, white below, their margins rolled back. The small two-lipped flowers in dense clusters at the ends of short shoots vary from pale greyish blue to clear blue. Usually it forms dense rounded bushes with laterally spreading branches, but the cultivar 'Fastigiatus' ('Miss Jessop's Upright') is of erect growth. 'Benenden Blue', with bright blue flowers, is a form of the Corsican variety *angustifolius*. (see p. 2)

The species inhabits dry scrub in the Mediterranean region

from the Balkan Peninsula to Spain and Portugal. In cultivation it is often severely damaged by cold spring gales and should be given a warm sheltered place in full sun, preferably against a south wall on a well-drained limy soil. Young vigorous plants survive adverse conditions better than old very woody bushes. If left unpruned rosemary tends to become straggling and short lived. The more straggling branches should be cut back each year in spring, but never beyond a growing shoot. Pruned plants will remain bushy and their life will be considerably prolonged. After 6 or 7 years the bushes become very woody at the base and lose vigour. Straggling branches will respond to hard pruning but replacement with young plants is recommended. This should be anticipated by inserting half ripe cuttings with a heel (with a sliver of the main stem attached) in open ground 1 or 2 years before the expected replanting. They can be taken at any time during July, August and September.

On heavy badly drained soils, rosemary can be grown in a tub or large pot in a sunny corner. Should the winter be severe, the container may be protected with sacking.

Rosemary was introduced into England in the fourteenth century for medicinal purposes. 'The rough refreshing scent of Rosemary, with its suggestion of nutmeg and pine-needles', as described by Boulestin and Hill, together with its strong taste, make it valuable for flavouring many dishes, including eggs, fish, soups and vegetables, but it should be used sparingly. Meat and poultry are often laced with short soft shoots; they can be chopped and added to stuffing or a bouquet inserted into the cavity of a chicken before roasting or boiling. (see p. 39)

Rue

Ruta graveolens L.   Rutaceae

Rue is a hardy evergreen shrub which makes a neat rounded bush rarely more than 2 feet (60 cm) high, with elegant rather thick grey or bluish leaves pinnately divided into somewhat wedge-shaped segments, rounded or indented at the ends. The yellow flowers are interesting but not particularly attractive. The leaves have a strong smell when crushed and a strong flavour; hence not more than a few finely chopped leaves should be added to sandwiches and salads. It is a native of the Balkan Peninsula but, having been cultivated for many centuries and seeding freely, it has become naturalised elsewhere. Self-sown seedlings arise near plants which have been allowed to fruit: it is also easily propagated by cuttings. When growing on fertile soils the growth tends to be loose and open. The compact and neat shape can be maintained by an annual clipping over with shears in March. Rue was much used as a medicinal herb in olden times; it is now grown mainly for its attractive appearance. The flower spikes should be removed as soon as they appear.

Sage

Salvia officinalis L.   Labiatae (Lamiaceae)

The common sage comes from arid stony places in southern Europe and, like most plants of this provenance, does best in cultivation when given a position in full sun sheltered from cold winds. It is a small shrub not more than 2 feet (30 cm) high with a tough woody stem and soft annual growth, bearing persistent oblong stalked pointed leaves with finely toothed margins and of greyish velvety appearance, the blades up to 2 inches (5 cm) long and $\frac{3}{4}$ inch (2 cm) broad. The commonly cultivated broad-leaved English sage rarely flowers and hence is preferred by commercial herb growers. The flowers of other forms, typically purple but white in 'Alba', are freely produced about $\frac{1}{2}$ to $\frac{3}{4}$ inch (12 to 20 mm) long, in loose spikes terminating annual growth and are quite decorative.

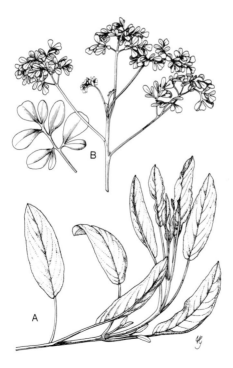

A. Sage (*Salvia officinalis*). B. Rue (*Ruta graveolens*).

Common sage, *Salvia officinalis*, (see previous page).

There are several forms differing in leaf colour from the typical 'sage-green' form; those most frequently grown are 'Purpurascens' with purplish leaves, 'Icterina' with yellow edged leaves, 'Tricolor' with grey leaves with variegated with white, purple and pink. These are not as hardy as the common sage and because they age quickly must be renewed more frequently. They make spreading mounds and are suitable for the front of the border and as ground cover. They are best renewed after 4 to 5 years when they will have become untidy. They are readily propagated by heaping sandy soil on the bush in March, shaking it down to leave the upper parts of the shoots clear. These will root below and can be divided and replanted in a rainy period in late summer.

When flowering is finished in July all the sages should be cut back lightly into current year's growth, never into the hard woody branches unless these are making new growth lower down. The non-flowering types also need pruning at this time, to allow sufficient time for the new growth to ripen before the approach of winter.

Propagation is by soft wood cuttings taken in April or May and set in a cold frame, by heel cuttings in a well drained soil in the open, or as described earlier for the forms with low prostrate growth.

Sage is very strongly and distinctively flavoured and counteracts the richness of fat meats, but, as stated by Boulestin and Hill, 'Sage should be used sparingly in the stuffing of duck or goose, as its flavour and its scent are overpowering and likely to kill the taste of anything else, including that of the bird stuffed'. It is a popular flavouring for sausages and certain cheeses. A few leaves of sage laid on cutlets or joints of pork or veal add a delicious flavour and pieces of eel can be wrapped in them for the last stage of cooking.

Savory

Satureja hortensis L. (Summer savory)   Labiatae (Lamiaceae)
Satureja montana L. (Winter savory)

Summer savory is a minutely hairy erect slender annual about 6 to 12 inches high (15 to 30 cm), with blunt linear leaves and small purplish or almost white flowers in the axils of the leaves. It is a native of the Mediterranean region and requires a light rich soil and a sunny position. Usually it is sown in April where it is to grow, the seedlings being thinned to 6 inches (15 cm) apart, and

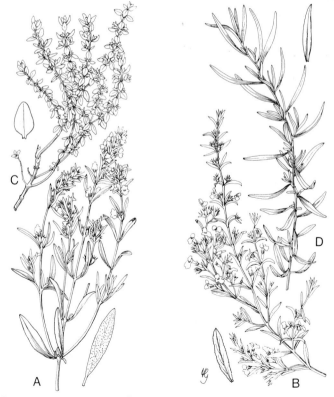

A. Summer savory (*Satureja hortensis*). B. Winter savory (*Satureja montana*). C. Thyme (*Thymus vulgaris*). D. Tarragon (*Artemisia dracunculus*).

providing shoots for cutting from June until the first frost: they make small leafy bushes. Once this herb has been grown self-sown seedlings appear every year, and these will transplant easily. The flavour is strong, somewhat like marjoram, so only small amounts should be added to any dish. It enhances the flavour of all green beans, especially broad beans, and a few leafy shoots can be added when these are being prepared for the freezer.

Winter savory is a woody perennial native to southern Europe. It makes a pleasing little bush about a foot (30 cm) high with small pointed mostly linear leaves and small purplish or almost white flowers in the axils of the leaves. It can be grown in poor soil as an edging or in the rock garden. The taller upright forms grown in the herb garden should be cut back to the woody base each spring to encourage new sappy shoots, usually a foot high for culinary use. Cuttings with a woody heel will quickly root in the open in a well-drained soil. It has a stronger and more pungent and less palatable flavour than summer savory and hence is rarely used for flavouring on its own but included in mixed herbs for its hot spiciness.

Sorrel

Rumex acetosa L. (Common Sorrel)   Polygonaceae
Rumex rugosus Campdera (Garden Sorrel)
Rumex scutatus (French Sorrel)

The sorrels are kinds of dock with sharp-tasting foliage used in the making of soup, for which the garden sorrel, R. rugosus (R. ambiguus Grenier) is best as it is less acid. This is a herbaceous perennial of unknown origin. The large long-stalked leaves have slightly puckered blades like blunt arrowheads, being 2–4 times as long as broad. The flowering stems, with numerous ascending branches and very small flowers, may rise to about $3\frac{1}{2}$ feet (1.05 m.). To get succulent growth the plants should be spaced 15 to 18 inches (38 to 45 cm) apart on well-manured non-calcareous soil and kept well-watered. Propagation is either by dividing plants in autumn or sowing seed in late March where the plants are to grow.

The French sorrel, R. scutatus, has a wide distribution in Europe and Western Asia and was introduced into Britain long ago, presumably from France, as a culinary plant, becoming naturalised here and there. It makes a tangled mass of leafy stems, with the small blunt leaf-blades about as long as broad. The flowering stem has few branches and grows to about $1\frac{1}{2}$ feet (45 cm).

Common sorrel, R. acetosa, is widespread on acid soils in the British Isles and over most of the Continent. It grows usually between 17 inches (45 cm) and 3 feet (100 cm). The leaf blades, shaped somewhat like arrowheads, are much longer than broad. A selected form of this species is sometimes used as a herb but is very acid and may cause stomach upset. Large leaves can be wrapped around a joint of meat as a tenderizer.

There is much confusion over the common names of these two sorrels and they are frequently interchanged. By some authors the above three species have been placed in a genus *Acetosa* as *A. rugosa*, *A. scutatus* and *A. pratensis*. They may be distinguished as follows:

1. Leaf-blades about as broad as long, French Sorrel (*R. scutatus*)
1. Leaf-blades 2–4 times as long as broad...   2
2. Leaf-blades 1–5 cm broad. Inflorescence with few branches...
   Common Sorrel (*R. acetosa*)
2. Leaf-blades 6–10 cm broad. Inflorescence with many branches...   Garden Sorrel (*R. rugosus*)

Sorrel leaves may be wrapped around meat as a tenderiser.

Sweet Cicely

Myrrhis odorata L.   Umbelliferae (Apiaceae)

The usual English name of this pleasantly scented and decorative herb, sometimes shortened to Sweet Cis, refers not to some nice forgotten girl but derives from the Greek *seseli*, which is now used for a different genus of Umbelliferae; in northern England it has also been called anise and annaseed in allusion to the distinct aniseed flavour of the leaves and fruits. It is a long-lived herbaceous perennial with a large thick rootstock and wide-spreading soft much divided fern-like leaves, some up to 2 feet (60 cm) long and 1 foot (30 cm) wide, white-flecked. The erect much-branched flowering stems from 2 to 5 feet (60 to 150 cm) high carry many umbels of small white flowers in May and June, followed by narrow sharply ridged fruits which become dark brown when ripe. As with many umbellifers, it is well to remove most if not all of these before they ripen to prevent self-sown seedlings becoming a nuisance.

Sweet cicely is native to the mountains of southern Europe but

Sweet cicely, *Myrrhis odorata*, a herb that has become naturalised in many places in Great Britain.

has become completely naturalised in damp places in many parts of the British Isles, particularly northern England and southern Scotland. It will grow in most conditions but grows most luxuriantly in half-shade on a moist soil. It seeds freely. The roots may be carefully divided in spring or autumn.

The leaves and young fruits can be chewed for their aniseed flavour, or the leaf-stalks chopped and added to acid fruits to reduce the amount of sugar required in cooking. Finely chopped leaves can also be added to strawberries. The roots of young plants can be boiled and eaten with salads.

Tarragon
Artemisia dracunculus L.   Compositae (Asteraceae)
Tarragon is a moderately hardy herbaceous perennial with spreading underground runners and slender erect branched stems bearing widely spaced, alternate, narrow linear leaves and very small flowerheads. The leaves are entire, not divided as in most species of *Artemisia*. It has two forms, very similar in appearance but markedly different in flavour, known as true or French tarragon (var. *sativa*) and Russian tarragon (var. *inodora*) also known as *A. dracunculoides*.

French tarragon, described by Claire Loewenfeld as 'probably the king of all culinary herbs', has a distinctive flavour unlike that of any other herb. Chopped leaves are used sparingly in salads, on potatoes, and in many dishes, notably chicken. Tarragon vinegar is made by steeping the young shoots and leaves in wine vinegar for at least 14 days.

The plant grows about $2\frac{1}{2}$ to 3 feet (1 m), with leaves up to 3 inches (7.5 cm) long and $\frac{1}{2}$ inch (1.3 cm) wide. It needs a sunny position and well-drained soil; plenty of well decayed humus should be added to the soil to make this retentive of moisture during the growing period. It should be divided and replanted in fresh soil about every four years in early spring just as the new growth is seen, the short white brittle rhizomes being lifted carefully and teased out. If this replanting is omitted the plants become crowded with growth and will deteriorate and the delicate flavour will be lost. French tarragon produces no seed, but it can be increased by removing shoots 10 inches (25 cm) long with a small piece of root attached and treating them as half-ripe cuttings. Its origin is somewhat uncertain but is apparently southern European Russia.

Russian tarragon is a more vigorous and hardier plant reaching a height of 6 feet (2 m) but has little flavour and that unpleasant. Indeed it is a waste of space to grow this when French tarragon is available.

Above: French tarragon (*Artemisia dracunculus* var. *sativa*) is a fairly hardy herbaceous perennial with leaves that have a distinctive flavour which particularly enhances the taste of chicken.

Left: Tarragon flowers; no seed is produced.

Thyme

Thymus   Labiatae (Lamiaceae)
T. × citriodorus (Persoon) Schreber (Lemon thyme)
T. *herba-barona* Loisel. (Caraway thyme)
T. *vulgaris* L. (Garden thyme)
The genus *Thymus* is botanically a very complicated group, of
which 66 European species, as well as numerous subspecies, are
described in the *Flora Europaea* (1972); the *R.H.S. Dictionary of
Gardening* (1951) describes 35 horticulturally interesting species
and hybrids. Although these have distinctive odours and flavours,
only three are grown for culinary use.

Garden thyme (T. *vulgaris*), also known as common or French
thyme, is derived from a low bushy species common on mountain
slopes in the west Mediterranean region. The cultivated form is a
shrublet of stiff compact evergreen habit rarely more than 9
inches (23 cm) high, with stiff ascending shoots bearing numerous
deep green leaves, $\frac{1}{5}$ to $\frac{3}{5}$ inch long (5–15 mm) with reflexed
margins, closely hairy below; the shoots end in loose interrupted
spikes of small, pale lilac-mauve flowers. It should be grown in
full sun; the ideal soil is stony and calcareous but it will grow on
any well-drained soil. As soon as the flowers fade, the plants
should be trimmed to encourage new growth for kitchen use.

Lemon thyme (T. × citriodorus) is a hybrid derived from T.
pulegioides (T. *chamaedrys*) and T. *vulgaris*. It makes a looser and
more open bush than garden thyme, up to a foot (30 cm) high, with
somewhat broader leaves usually hairless below, and has a
distinct lemon scent. It flowers later and the flowers are a deeper
pink. It needs an open soil with plenty of humus to retain
moisture but is less hardy than garden thyme and may die in a wet
cold winter. There are various forms of lemon thyme including
one of spreading mat-like growth 4 to 6 inches (10 to 15 cm) high
with deep yellow leaves.

   Both garden thyme and lemon thyme can be increased by
cuttings and by division. Division is easily done if, during the
previous spring, sandy soil is piled into the centre of the plant up
to the level of the young growth. By the following spring roots will
have formed on the buried wood and the small well-rooted shoots
can be separated. Many self-sown seedlings may be found around
a plant of garden thyme but these are likely to be inferior in
flavour to the carefully selected original strain. It has a strong
aroma and hence should be used sparingly, being preferred for
mutton, pork and eels; it is always added to mixed herbs and is an
essential ingredient of *bouquet garni*. Those who find the flavour
of garden thyme too dominating may prefer the milder and fruity

flavour of lemon thyme, which is sometimes added to a baked custard.

Caraway thyme (*T. herba-barona*) is a low-growing plant with ascending or arching shoots which root as they come in contact with the soil and form a loose mat with ovate or lanceolate leaves to $\frac{3}{10}$ inch (8 mm) long, the pale pink flowers being borne in hemispherical or oblong heads. It is a native of Sardinia and Corsica; *herba barona* is a Corsican vernacular name. Its aroma reminds one of caraway as well as of thyme; hence it can be used to give a different and subtle flavour to food.

A corner of a herb garden showing the feathery leaves of fennel, and mint.

SOME BOOKS FOR FURTHER INFORMATION

BACK, ARABELLA & BACK, PHILIPPA. 1980. *The Herb Book*. London (Octopus Books).

BOULESTIN, X. M. & HILL, JASON (F. A. HAMPTON). 1930. *Herbs, Salads and Seasonings*. London

BROWNLOW, MARGARET E. 1978. *Herbs and the Fragrant Garden*. 3rd ed. London (Darton, Longman and Todd)

CARRUTHERS, BARBARA. 1981. *The Herb Growers Guide*. London (Warne).

CLARKSON, ROSETTA E. 1942. *Herbs, their culture and uses*. New York (Macmillan).

CROCKETT, JAMES & OTHERS. 1979. *Herbs* London etc. (Time-Life Books).

DAISLEY, GILDA. 1982. *The illustrated Book of Herbs*. London (Ebury Press).

DAMPNEY, JANET & POMEROY, ELIZABETH. 1977. *All about Herbs*. London etc. (Hamlyn).

DAVID, ELIZABETH. *Herbs, Spices, Salt and Aromatics in the English Kitchen*. Harmondsworth (Penguin Books)

FLOWER, BARBARA & ROSENBAUM, ELISABETH. 1958. *Apicii Artis Magiricae Libri* x. *The Roman Cookery Book, a critical Translation of the Art of Cooking by Apicius*. London (George G. Harrap)

FOSTER, GERTRUDE. 1975. *Herbs for every Garden*. 2nd ed. London (J. M. Dent), New York (E. P. Dutton)

GENDERS, ROY. 1980. *The complete Book of Herbs and Herb Growing*. London (Ward Lock).

HALL, DOROTHY. 1976. *The Book of Herbs* London & Sydney (Pan Books).

HEMPHILL, JOHN & HEMPHILL, ROSEMARY. 1983. *Herbs, their Cultivation and Usage*. Poole (Blandford Press).

HEMPHILL, ROSEMARY. 1968. *Herbs and Spices*. Harmondsworth (Penguin Books)

HEMPHILL, JOHN and ROSEMARY. 1972. *Herbs for all seasons*. Harmondsworth (Penguin Books).

LOWENFELD, CLAIRE , 1984. *Herb Gardening; why and how to grow Herbs*. London (Faber & Faber). A highly recommended practical work, including culinary use.

LOEWENFELD, CLAIRE & BACK, PHILIPPA. 1971. *Herbs for Health and Cookery*. London (Pan Books)

LOEWENFELD, CLAIRE & BACK, PHILIPPA. 1978. *The Complete Book of Herbs and Spices*. 2nd edition Newton Abbot (David & Charles)

MACLEOD, DAWN. 1968. *A Book of Herbs*. London (Duckworth).

MAWSON, MONICA. 1972. *Herb and Spice Cookery*. 2nd edition London (Hamlyn)

PAGE, MARY. 1980. *The Observer's Book of Herbs* London (Warne).

PEPLOW, ELIZABETH & PEPLOW, REGINALD. 1984. *Herbs and Herb Gardens of Great Britain*. Exeter (Webb & Bower).

RHODE, ELEANOUR S. 1926. *A Garden of Herbs*. 2nd ed. London (Jenkins).

ROSENGARTEN, F. 1969. *The Book of Spices*. Wynnewood, Pennsylvania (Macrae Smith Co. for Livingston Publishing Co.) A sumptuous profusely illustrated work

RUTHERFORD, MEG. 1975. *A Pattern of Herbs*. London (Allen & Unwin).

SANECKI, KAY N. 1974. *The Complete Book of Herbs*. London (Macdonald)

SANECKI, KAY N. 1978. *Discovering Herbs*. New impress. Princes Risborough (Shire Publications)

STOBART, T. 1970. *Herbs, Spices and Flavourings*. Newton Abbott (David & Charles).

STUART, MALCOLM (Ed.). 1979. *The Encyclopedia of Herbs and Herbalism*. London (Orbis).

WALKDEN, BRIAN & WALKDEN, MAY. 1979. *Growing and Storing Herbs*. Wellingborough, Northamptonshire (Thorsons).

THE BRITISH MUSEUM (Natural History) at South Kensington London, has published a wallchart (BS 1) illustrating culinary herbs in colour.

The above list is far from exhaustive. Many interesting short articles on herbs will be found in *The Herbalist* published annually by The Herb Society of America, Boston, Mass. in *The Herb Quarterly* published quarterly by Uphill Press, Newpane Vermont and especially notable for recipes and in *The Herbal Review* published quarterly by The Herb Society, London; the latter has also published booklets on chives, mints, parsley and rosemary.